Church Chuckles

It's income tax time so remember what the Bible says: Beware of false profits.

Every Day Thoughts™

new seasons®

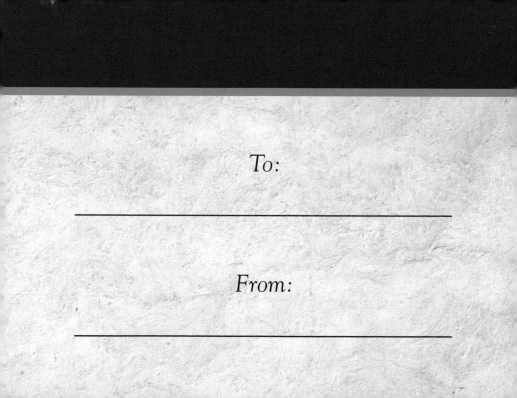

To:

_____

From:

_____

Dates to Remember

CHURCH NOTES

A Teen Dance Social will be held in the gymnasium next Friday at 7:30 P.M. All teenagers must be at least 13 years old.

Anniversary Gifts

First	Paper	Thirteenth	Lace
Second	Cotton	Fourteenth	Ivory
Third	Leather	Fifteenth	Crystal
Fourth	Fruit/Flowers	Twentieth	China
Fifth	Wood	Twenty-fifth	Silver
Sixth	Candy/Iron	Thirtieth	Pearl
Seventh	Wool/Copper	Thirty-fifth	Coral
Eighth	Bronze/Pottery	Fortieth	Ruby
Ninth	Pottery/Willow	Forty-fifth	Sapphire
Tenth	Tin/Aluminum	Fiftieth	Gold
Eleventh	Steel	Fifty-fifth	Emerald
Twelfth	Silk/Linen	Sixtieth	Diamond

"*I* hope you saved your receipts," Quentin told the groom before the wedding. "My dad said you have to exchange your vows."

December
Birthdays & Anniversaries

Birthstone: Turquoise
Flower: Poinsettia

January 4

Lisa came home from Sunday school and told her mother that she had learned a new song about a cross-eyed bear named Gladly. It took her mother awhile before she realized that the hymn was really "Gladly the Cross I'd Bear."

November
Birthdays & Anniversaries

_____   _____

_____   _____

_____   _____

_____   _____

_____   _____

_____   _____

_____   _____

Birthstone: Topaz
Flower: Chrysanthemum

CHURCH EVENTS

For next week's men's clothing drive we are requesting you drop your pants in the basement.

October
Birthdays & Anniversaries

Birthstone: Opal
Flower: Dahlia

Dear God,
I went to this
wedding and they
kissed right in
church. Is that
okay?

NEIL, AGE 8

September
Birthdays & Anniversaries

Birthstone: Sapphire
Flower: Aster

January 7

CHURCH HAPPENINGS

*B*ecause of our special silent devotional service, the pastor asks that you leave all crying babies at home.

August
Birthdays & Anniversaries

....

....

....

....

....

....

....

Birthstone: Peridot
Flower: Gladiolus

January 8

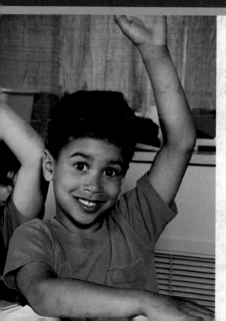

"Why did Moses have to go back up the mountain a second time?" asked the Sunday school teacher.

"To ask God for a map," Brad replied.

July
Birthdays & Anniversaries

Birthstone: Ruby
Flower: Sweet Pea

January 9

Emily's mother asked her what they were supposed to do before each meal.

Emily replied, "We braise the Lord and thank him for the food."

June

Birthdays & Anniversaries

Birthstone: Pearl
Flower: Rose

January 10

Dear God,
I read the Bible.
What does "begat"
mean? Nobody will
tell me.

ALISON, AGE 9

May
Birthdays & Anniversaries

Birthstone: Emerald
Flower: Lily of the Valley

SERVICE NOTES

Anyone who has lost their job recently is invited to attend a special service on Monday evening to join together and pray to a hire power.

April
Birthdays & Anniversaries

Birthstone: Diamond
Flower: Daisy or Lily

"Grandma, was Noah's wife called Joan of Ark?"

March
Birthdays & Anniversaries

Birthstone: Aquamarine
Flower: Violet

January 13

This afternoon there will be meetings in the South and North ends of the church. Children will be baptized at both ends.

February
Birthdays & Anniversaries

Birthstone: Amethyst
Flower: Primrose

January 14

CHURCH HAPPENINGS

Our soloist has returned from having reconstructive surgery. The choir is happy to welcome her back with a joyful nose.

January
Birthdays & Anniversaries

Birthstone: Garnet
Flower: Carnation

January 15

At an atheist funeral: "Here lies an atheist, all dressed up and nowhere to go."

December 31

Dear Pastor,
How does God know the good people from the bad people? Do you tell him, or does he read it in the newspapers?

ADAM, AGE 6

January 16

VOLUNTEER OPPORTUNITIES

We need one more player on the church soccer team. Ask yourself: "Am I my brother's goalkeeper?"

December 30

CHURCH NOTES

Church deacons are not to pass out until the Pastor finishes preaching.

January 17

Dear Pastor,
I'm sorry I couldn't leave more money in the plate. Could you please have a sermon about a raise in my allowance?

STEPHANIE, AGE 10

December 29

Baptismal pool repairs have been postponed for a week because Reverend Atkins has been feeling under the water.

January 18

Jessica walked up to the pastor and asked, "Were the epistles the wives of the apostles?"

*F*ather Joe tried to appeal to the baby boomers in church when he said, "Some of you on the stairway to heaven need to start praying for an elevator."

January 19

Josh was trying to teach his puppy to walk alongside him by reading the Bible to him. When asked why, he said, "I'm using the heeling power of prayer."

Dear God,
The bad people laughed at Noah and said, "You made an ark on dry land, silly." But Noah was smart and he stuck with you. That's what I would do.

WILLIAM, AGE 7

January 20

Dear God,
I would like to live
900 years like that
guy in the Bible.

JASON, AGE 9

December 26

Flowers for Sunday's services were donated by Smith Chrysler Plymouth. Mrs. Smith will also be the choir's guest soloist, singing "A Mighty Fortress Is Our Dodge."

January 21

SERVICE NOTES

The blessing of the pets will be followed by a hot dog lunch.

December 25

OUR CHURCH TODAY

After eating Christmas dinner, join us in the church hall for a Christmas concert. The choir will open with "O Come All Ye Facefull."

January 22

December 24

*L*ittle Wayne could always be found sitting under the Christmas tree singing his favorite song: "A Wayne in the Manger."

January 23

*B*efore sending shipments of bottled water to people who have not yet found God, Reverend Peter will pray for their salivation.

December 23

Mark explained to his parents, "Jesus used to fly on an airplane, and Pontius was the pilot!"

PASTOR UPS AND DOWNS

Good news: The Women's Guild voted to send you a get-well card.
Bad news: The vote passed 31–30.

December 22

Dear God,
Please send me a
pony. I never asked
for anything before.
You can look it up.

Bruce, age 7

Malcolm, the ring bearer, walked up to the minister as he was preparing for the marriage service and asked why he wasn't wearing his bulletproof vest. "You need to be careful," he told him. "My dad said this was going to be a shotgun wedding."

December 21

Ray carefully folded a paper airplane and put it next to the figure on the top of the Christmas tree. "He's a Blue Angel," he explained.

January 26

Father Craig hated when marriage ceremonies were interrupted by picture-taking, so he told the congregation: "Even if your spirit is willing, let your flash be weak."

December 20

Church sign that's peeling:

Sinners
Repaint!

After Bobby's pet bird died, he decided it needed a proper funeral. He held a wonderful service in the backyard and concluded with, "Ashes to ashes, ducks to ducks."

SERVICE NOTES

*L*adies' Bible Study will be held Thursday morning at 10:00. All ladies are invited to lunch in the Fellowship Hall after the B.S. is over.

January 28

OUR CHURCH TODAY

The lecture on the religious history of circumcision has been cut from tonight's program.

December 18

When the Israelites left, the Egyptians tried to catch them racing through the dessert.

*R*everend Jerome will discuss the health risks of obesity, then the choir will sing "There's a Wideness in God's Mercy."

December 17

"My pastor says you must love your neighbor, even if you hate him."

A little boy was attending his first wedding. After the service, his cousin asked him, "How many women can a man marry?"

"Sixteen," the boy responded.

His cousin was amazed that he had an answer so quickly. "How do you know that?" he asked.

"Easy," the little boy said. "All you have to do is add it up, like the pastor said: four better, four worse, four richer, four poorer."

December 16

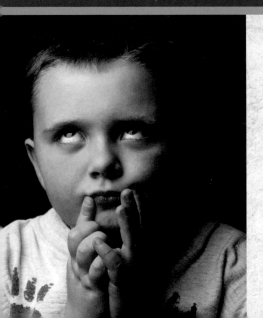

Blake gave the little figure hovering over the manger a tiny flashlight to hold. He said it was the "security guardian angel."

January 31

Dear Pastor,
I think a lot more people would probably come to your church if you moved it to Disneyland.

LAUREN, AGE 9

December 15

VOLUNTEER OPPORTUNITIES

The director of the Christmas pageant is still looking for wise men. No experience necessary.

February 1

VOLUNTEER OPPORTUNITIES

*F*ood drive next Sunday: All are requested to bring their cans to the back of the church.

December 14

Nick was competitive in everything he did. While the other kids were content to make snow angels, he would hold a toy sword in one hand and make snow archangels.

February 2

Sign on laundromat next door to a church: Here's where cleanliness really is next to godliness!

SERVICE NOTES

Let us give thanks to Susan Lewis for donating an organ to our music department.

February 3

The bride nearly fainted when Reverend Hal asked, "Do you, Robert, take Melinda to be your awful wedded wife?"

December 12

*E*mily was having a little difficulty with the Lord's prayer: "Our Father, who does art in heaven...."

CHURCH NOTES

Please put your donation along with any suggestions in the correction basket.

December 11

Guarding the front of the nativity scene under the Christmas tree was a small armored figure with tape over its mouth. When asked who it was, Kyle said, "That's the silent knight!"

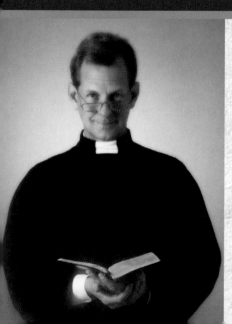

There's no bigger boxing fan than Father O'Conner. He always calls his favorite book about hell "Don King's Inferno."

December 10

After setting up the manger scene, the congregation will join us in singing "The First Motel."

"*I* know what a beatitude is," said Eva. "It's what makes bees buzz."

December 9

Dear God,
If you watch me in church Sunday, make sure you check out my new shoes.

MICKEY, AGE 8

February 7

The Sunday school teacher asked her class if anyone could recite the tenth commandment. Susie raised her hand, stood tall, and said, "Thou shalt not take the covers off thy neighbor's wife."

December 8

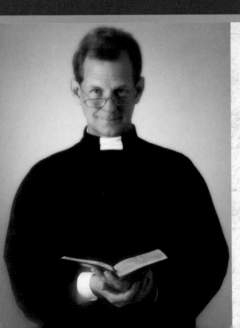

Next Sunday, Mrs. Benson will be soloist for the morning service. The pastor will then speak on "Hell on Earth."

February 8

ACKNOWLEDGMENTS

The Thank you to Bob's Markct, who gave substantial support during our food drive. As an added thanks, we ask you to patronize him for your grocery needs.

VOLUNTEER OPPORTUNITIES

The church choir will begin practice for the Christmas Cantata next Wednesday at 7:00 P.M. We have a special need for men's voices, but all parts are welcome.

February 9

*I*n Wednesday's prayer group, Steve Phillips will read his speech "Loving One Another: Excepting Those of Other Cultures."

December 6

Overheard at Sunday school: "Lot's wife never made her bed, so God turned her into a pillow of salt."

February 10

The Golfer's Hymn:
"There's a Green Hill
Far Away"

December 5

After Sunday school Nathan asked his mom, "Why would Jesus want 12 opossums?"

February 11

Dear Pastor,
I would like to go to heaven one day because I know my brother won't be there.

ANGELA, AGE 8

December 4

SERVICE NOTES

Miss Charlene Mason sang "I Will Not Pass this Way Again," which brought great joy to the congregation.

February 12

SERVICE NOTES

*I*f you, or someone close to you, are challenged by illness and are having a difficult time coping, please join our support group. Meetings are Thursday evenings at 7:00 in the back room of The Old Towne Pub.

December 3

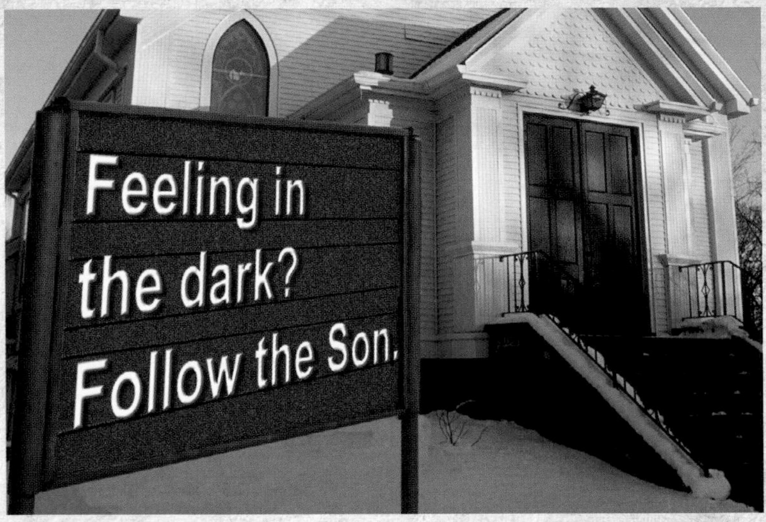

Over the massive front doors of a church, these words were inscribed: "The Gates of Heaven." Below that was a small cardboard sign saying, "Please use basement entrance."

December 2

CHURCH HAPPENINGS

Will all of those with rolls in the church Christmas play please report to the kitchen after the service.

February 14

We have been experiencing some problems with our church elevator. If it stops between floors, do not become alarmed. Simply press the "Alarm" button, and we will contact a maintenance person.

December 1

The Diet Club will meet Thursday night at 7:30. Please use the large double door at the side entrance.

"*I* think the richest animal is the mink," Lisa told her best friend. "I heard in church that the mink shall inherit the earth."

November 30

Dear God,
I think about you
sometimes, even when
I'm not praying.

HENRY, AGE 4

February 16

Our guest speaker is a prison minister who will talk about Christian felonship.

November 29

Sign on a fruit stand run by monks: "Amazing Grapes."

February 17

*T*he team knew what Reverend Oscar expected when he put his hand on the football during the pregame prayer and said, "This too shall pass."

November 28

Reverend Calvin's mother runs a gas station. One row of pumps has a sign that says, "Full service." The other row of pumps says, "God helps those that help themselves."

VOLUNTEER OPPORTUNITIES

This week our church will be collecting the following items: kitchen matches and school textbooks.

November 27

CHURCH NOTES

This Tuesday at 8:00 P.M. John Furley will read his prayer: "Ethics: Tips for Taking the Moral High Ground." This reading will be held in the church basement.

February 19

Wednesday at 5:00 P.M. there will be a meeting of the Little Mothers' Club. All wishing to become Little Mothers, please see the minister in his study.

Sign on the church lavatory:

Amen's Room

February 20

SERVICE NOTES

After the Ladies' Association potluck dinner, we will take a moment to pray for the sick.

Our pastor says, "You can call me Doc. I'm your holy plastic surgeon, here to give you a faith lift."

February 21

"God was the first police officer," said Nancy, "because on the seventh day he arrested."

November 24

Thursday night:
potluck dinner.
Prayer and
medication
to follow.

February 22

CHURCH HAPPENINGS

Attention Elders and Deacons:
The annual church bored meeting will be held Tuesday at 6:00 P.M.

November 23

SERVICE NOTES

The pastor welcomes you to the blessing of the pets. He will greet you in the church barking lot.

February 23

Oﬀertory: "Jesus Paid it All!"

Billy was using his father's drill on his new copy of the Good Book. He said it was because he got a Bible but what he wanted was the holey scriptures.

CHURCH NEWS

Many of you have mentioned that it is difficult to hear in church. We will be remodeling this summer; hopefully the agnostics will improve.

November 21

Dear God,
You don't have
to worry about me.
I always look both
ways.

MELANIE, AGE 7

February 25

Sign on the dairy case at a Christian grocery store:

I am my butter's keeper.

November 20

OUR CHURCH TODAY

Please welcome Carl Kilpatrick to our congregation. His telephone number is 444-436-8729, but he has requested we keep this private.

February 26

As the Sunday school teacher described how Lot's wife looked back and was turned into a pillar of salt, little Jimmy interrupted, "My mommy looked back once while she was driving, and she turned into a telephone pole!"

November 19

"This homework is too much for dial-a-prayer," Ellen complained. "What's the number for dial-a-whole-church?"

February 27

*E*ight new choir robes are currently needed due to the addition of several new members and to the deterioration of some of the older ones.

November 18

As several churchgoers got up to prepare for a buffet lunch, our minister announced, "The ladies leaving the sanctuary will have some hot buns for us after the service."

February 28

"Yes, Joseph and Mary were traveling to Nazareth," Reverend Martin responded to a question from a young man in his Bible study class, "but I don't think they would have called it a weekend getaway."

CHURCH NEWS

The vote to turn off the heat during the week to save gas has been passed.

HYMNS FOR THE AGING:
"Just a Slower Walk with Thee"
"Blessed Insurance"
"Count Your Many Birthdays,
Name Them One by One"

March 1

Our pastor will be attending a weekend seminar on mental illnesses. Please pray for his sane return.

November 15

Dear God,
Why is Sunday
school on Sunday?
I thought it was
supposed to be our
day of rest.

ANDREA, AGE 6

March 2

OUR CHURCH TODAY

Barbara Green remains in the hospital and needs blood donors for another transfusion. She is also having trouble sleeping and requests tapes of Pastor Jack's sermons.

November 14

*E*veryone knew what Reverend Joe's favorite sport was when he commented, "If I were a betting man, I'd take Daniel over the lions by 10."

March 3

Dear Pastor,
I know God loves everybody, but he never met my sister.

ARNOLD, AGE 7

November 13

ACKNOWLEDGMENTS

Phyllis Green would like to thank all of you who assisted her after her fall at last week's services. We are happy to report that the doctors X-rated her arms and legs and found no fractures.

VOLUNTEER OPPORTUNITIES

The church bowling team is looking for players. All skill levels welcome. Come join us even if you're in the gutter.

November 12

THE MORNING SERMON:
Gossip . . . The Speaking of Evil

THE EVENING SERMON:
I Love to Tell the Story

March 5

Little Johnny was crying on his way home from church. His father repeatedly asked him what was wrong. Johnny finally replied, "The preacher said he wanted us brought up in a Christian home, but I want to stay with you guys!"

November 11

Oscar must have been thinking about eating lunch when he asked his Sunday school teacher if Adam and Eve had a choice between original sin or extra crispy.

March 6

CHURCH NOTES

The church will host an evening of fine dining, superb entertainment, and gracious hostility.

CHURCH HAPPENINGS

The outreach committee has enlisted 25 visitors to call on people who are not already afflicted with another church.

"*I* know why Moses parted the Red Sea," Jill informed the class. "He was wearing a white robe and didn't want it to get any red stains."

November 9

The Meteorologist's Hymn: "There Shall Be Showers of Blessings"

March 8

CHURCH HAPPENINGS

Next Sunday is the family hayride and bonfire at the Johnson's. Everyone bring your own hot dogs and guns. Condiments and soda will be provided. Friends are welcome!

November 8

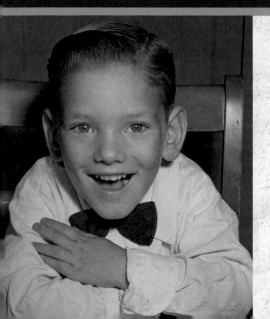

Dear Pastor,
Please say in your sermon that Jimmy Patterson has been a good boy all week. I am Jimmy Patterson.

JIMMY, AGE 7

March 9

*B*ouncing out of her first day at nursery school, a three-year-old girl gleefully informed her mother, "We had juice and Billy Graham crackers!"

November 7

"Let's sing that hymn about fishing," Pat told his Sunday school teacher. "You know, 'He's Got the Whole Worm in His Hands.'"

March 10

SERVICE NOTES

*F*or anyone donating adult gifts, see the church secretary.

CHURCH NOTES

Our church harp is making circles in the hardwood floor. Suggestions on how to get rid of these harp "O" marks are greatly appreciated.

March 11

"My baseball coach would want Abraham on his team," baseball expert Art told his friends, "because he obeyed the sign to sacrifice."

November 5

On their way to church service, a Sunday school teacher asked her pupils, "And why is it necessary to be quiet in church?"

One bright little girl replied, "Because people are sleeping."

March 12

OUR CHURCH TODAY

A men's-only worship group will be held Tuesday evenings at 7:00. Nancy Palmer will preside.

November 4

The pastor will preach his farewell message, after which the choir will sing, "Joy, Joy, Joy."

March 13

MORNING SERVICE:

Hymn 43: "Great God, What Do I Hear?"

Preacher: The Rev. Mark Mahoney.

Hymn 47: "Hark! An Awful Voice Is Sounding."

November 3

Q: Why do we say "Amen" at the end of a prayer instead of "Awomen"?

A: The same reason we sing Hymns instead of Hers!

March 14

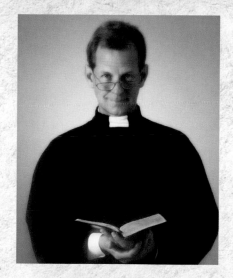

Deacon Steve always tried to look on the bright side. He said, "Pastor, I have some good news for you! Your biggest critic left the church. But the bad news is, he's been appointed your Head Bishop."

November 2

Brian's father asked him what he really liked about church. Brian thought about it a moment and replied, "The benediction."

March 15

There will be a rummage sale next Saturday. Ladies, please leave your clothes in the basement.

November 1

One evening Pastor Steve asked how many had read Mark 17, and every hand went up. The pastor said, "Mark has only 16 chapters. Let me begin my sermon on the sin of lying."

March 16

"The apocalypse will have a lot of yelling," Brian informed his father. "That's why there's going to be four hoarse men."

October 31

OUR CHURCH TODAY

The rosebud on the altar this morning is to announce the birth of David Alan Balser, the sin of Rev. and Mrs. Julius Balser.

March 17

The old church pipe organ had seen its better days. After one particularly out-of-tune song, the pastor turned to his assistant and said, "I don't know if we need an organ tuner or a plumber."

October 30

PASTOR UPS AND DOWNS

Good news: Church attendance rose dramatically the last three weeks. Bad news: You were on vacation.

March 18

Let us take a moment to remember those
around you who have died.

October 29

At the service before Halloween, Pastor Martha told the congregation not to put their faith in false gourds.

March 19

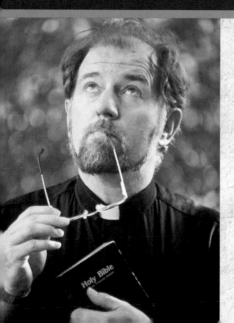

*R*everend Roy cared for both the body and the soul of his flock. That's why he told them: "And ye shall eat the monounsaturated and polyunsaturated fat of the land."

October 28

CHURCH HAPPENINGS

Please sign up to attend the Prayer and Fasting Conference. The cost of attending includes meals.

March 20

The congregation will sing "Savior, Like a Shepherd Lead Us"... if time permits.

October 27

Dear God,
I hope to go to
heaven someday,
but later rather
than sooner.

LOGAN, AGE 5

OUR CHURCH TODAY

The funeral for the late basketball coach was well attended, with former players filling the pews and current players acting as tall-bearers.

October 26

We will have a blessing of the pets after the 9:00 service. Dogs and cats first, other animals blessed after. Please keep birds, reptiles, rodents, and fish separrot.

March 22

"Grandpa should have been in the Garden of Eden instead of Adam," Jules told his mom. "He can't eat an apple without his false teeth."

October 25

A sign on a rehab company's truck:

Repaint, and thin no more!

March 23

CHURCH HAPPENINGS

*E*veryone is excited about the upcoming wedding of Brad and Melody. They are having a "country style" wedding, and everyone is invited to join them as they exchange cows in the church courtyard.

October 24

ACKNOWLEDGMENTS

The ladies of the church have cast-off clothing of every kind, and they can be seen in the church basement on Friday.

March 24

*R*everend Ryan was definitely on a diet when he said, "Be good, low-carb Christians and do not partake of the forbidden fruits."

October 23

A trio called The Resurrection was scheduled to sing at a church revival, but a storm postponed their performance. The pastor changed the sign outside to read:

The Resurrection has been postponed.

October 22

Dear God,
Instead of letting people die and having to make new ones, why don't you just keep the ones you already have?

KATHY, AGE 8

March 26

Amanda explained why she brought her dolls to Sunday school: "I'm building a Tower of Barbie."

October 21

Next Thursday there will be tryouts for the choir. Please come, they need all the help they can get.

March 27

OUR CHURCH TODAY

For Easter services, we will ask Mrs. Brown to come forward and lay an egg on the altar.

Happy Easter

October 20

The Sunday school teacher asked, "Now Thomas, tell me frankly, do you say a prayer before eating?"

"No, sir," Thomas replied, "I don't have to. My mom is a good cook."

March 28

Dear God,
I want to be just like my Daddy when I get big, but with not so much hair all over.

SAM, AGE 8

October 19

On a church bulletin during the minister's illness: "GOD IS GOOD! Dr. Harmon is better."

March 29

SERVICE NOTES

The visiting monster today is Reverend Jack Bains.

October 18

CHURCH NOTES

The church bulletin can now be viewed online. If you do not have a computer, e-mail Margaret and ask her to forward it to you.

March 30

Dear God,
Is it true my father
won't get into heaven
if he uses his bowling
words in the house?

JENNIFER, AGE 8

October 17

Dear God,
Are you really
invisible or is that
just a trick?

LUCY, AGE 4

CHURCH NEWS

Jean's weight-management series will be meeting on Wednesday nights. She's used the program herself and has been growing like crazy!

October 16

CHURCH NEWS

*D*ue to the rector's illness, Wednesday night healing services will be discontinued until further notice.

April 1

Church sign:

No shoes
No shirt
No service

October 15

SERVICE NOTES

During the absence of our pastor, we enjoyed the rare privilege of hearing a good sermon when Reverend Tom Kelly supplied our pulpit.

April 2

The concert held in Fellowship Hall was a great success. Special thanks are due to the minister's daughter, who labored the whole evening at the piano, which as usual fell on her.

October 14

Our pastor is a real comedian. He calls the Ten Commandments "God's Top Ten Signs You May Not Be Going to Heaven."

CHURCH HAPPENINGS

Sunday worship will begin with personal medication.

October 13

After the service, Johnny asked his mother, "In the preacher's sermon on Acts today he said the apostles were all in one Accord. Did they really have cars back then?"

April 4

Dear God,
I think the stapler is
one of your greatest
inventions.

RUTH, AGE 10

October 12

Please welcome
Pastor Donna, a caring
individual who loves
hurting people.

April 5

October 11

Dear God,
I thank you for my
baby brother, but
what I prayed for
was a puppy.

SCOTTIE, AGE 7

April 6

Our Church Today

*P*lease join us Saturday at 2:00 for our Annual Church Pot Lick. Details forthcoming!

October 10

The Sunday school teacher asked Sarah why she drew Jesus sitting on a horse.

Sarah replied, "He's giving his sermon on the mount."

April 7

Asked what she had learned during the service, Janet replied, "A Christian should have only one spouse. This is called monotony."

October 9

A pastor said to a precocious six-year-old boy, "So your mother says your prayers for you each night? Very commendable. What does she say?"

The little boy replied, "Thank God he's in bed!"

Dear Pastor,
My mother is very
religious. She goes to
play bingo at the
church every week
even if she has a cold.

ANNETTE, AGE 8

October 8

The rookie preacher got so flustered during his first sermon, he had to pull out his cell phone and call dial-a-prayer.

April 9

Johnny told his father, "If hell is more boring than church I promise to always be good."

October 7

A little girl became restless as the preacher's sermon dragged on and on. Finally, she leaned over to her mother and whispered, "Mommy, if we give him money now, will he let us go?"

April 10

CHURCH NOTES

We need volunteers for summer camp. There will be sinning and dancing.

October 6

Dear God,
It rained our whole
vacation and, boy, was
my father mad. He said
some things about you
that people are not
supposed to say, but
I hope you do not hurt
him anyway.

ANNA, AGE 4

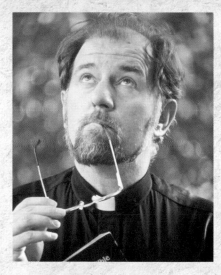

*R*everend Nichols must have known what effect his long sermons were having on the congregation when he accidentally referred to them as "bored-again Christians."

October 5

ACKNOWLEDGMENTS

The "Over-Sixties" choir will be disbanded for the winter with the thanks of the entire church.

April 12

VOLUNTEER OPPORTUNITIES

We're looking for volunteers for our prison ministry. You can help put the "con" in "congregation."

October 4

*F*ather Jeremy keeps up with all the latest diet crazes, including low-carb. He lets parishioners opt to say: "Give us this day our daily meat."

April 13

A Sunday school teacher asked his class why Joseph and Mary took Jesus with them to Jerusalem. One confident child replied, "They couldn't get a babysitter."

October 3

A little girl's prayer: "Dear God, please take care of Daddy and Mommy and my sister and my brother and me. And please take care of yourself, God. If anything happens to you, we're gonna be in a big mess."

We knew Reverend Smith was irritated by interruptions when he said, "In I Corinthians 7:20 we read: 'Let every man abide in the same calling wherein he was called'—except on his cell phone in church!"

October 2

CHURCH HAPPENINGS

Bilingual chicken dinner this Sunday at noon.

April 15

It's income tax time so remember what the Bible says: Beware of false profits.

October 1

Dear God,
I don't think anybody could be a better God. I just wanted you to know that. And I am not just saying that because you are God already.

BOBBY, AGE 4

April 16

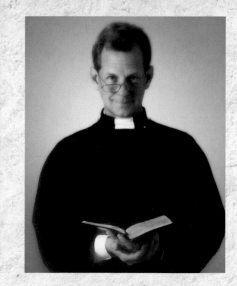

*F*ather Phil bent down to pick up his notes, and the entire church heard his pants rip. Red-faced, he looked up and said, "If anyone can pass a thread through the eye of a needle, I'll make it easier for them to get into the Kingdom of Heaven."

September 30

Make singing
a habit.

CHURCH HAPPENINGS

Next Saturday we will hold our semiannual Adult Personal Growth Workshop. Complimentary day care will be provided at a cost of $5 per child.

September 29

A bean supper will be held prior to our
Church Mission meeting. Music will follow.

April 18

Reverend Alex blessed the all-natural cereal being served at the vegetarian prayer breakfast, then told the attendants: "And now, let us be filled with the holy groats."

September 28

A preacher's little boy inquired, "Daddy, every Sunday when you first come out to preach, you sit on the platform and bow your head. What are you doing?"

The father explained, "I'm asking the Lord to give me a good sermon."

The little boy asked, "Why doesn't he?"

April 19

OUR CHURCH TODAY

We pray that our people will jumble themselves before God.

September 27

*I*f all of the pews are full when you arrive, please wait in the aisle for help from one of the pushers.

"God created two people instead of one or three," Alexis informed her mother, "because they lived in the Garden of Even."

September 26

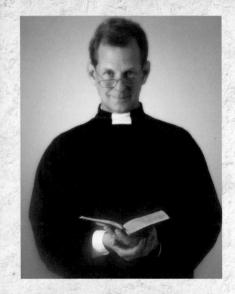

*R*everend Mike knew how to keep the attention of the congregation. During the fall he referred to Jesus serving the multitude with five loaves and two fish as a "biblical tailgate party."

April 21

CHURCH NEWS

Missing: a purple lady's bicycle from the church parking lot.

September 25

Don't let worry kill you.
The Church can help.

April 22

After watching the kids at the school party, Father Joel said, "There's a time to weep and a time to laugh, a time to mourn, and a time to dance. And I think I've seen them all tonight."

September 24

My wife and I invited several people to dinner. At the table, she turned to our eight-year-old daughter and said, "Would you like to say the blessing?"

"I wouldn't know what to say," she replied.

"Just say what you hear Mommy say," my wife encouraged.

Our daughter bowed her head and said, "Dear Lord, why on earth did I invite all these people to dinner?"

Dear God,
Is there any way to do extra credit to make sure I get into heaven?

BENJAMIN, AGE 8

September 23

Wednesday the ladies'
liturgy will meet.
Mrs. Johnson will sing
"Put Me in My Little Bed"
accompanied by the pastor.

April 24

Preacher Tina quoted Job 5:1: "Call now, if there be any that will answer thee." A voice in the back of the church replied, "Operators are standing by."

September 22

A little boy was overheard praying, "Lord, if you can't make me a better boy, don't worry about it. I'm having a real good time just as I am."

CHURCH NOTES

Attention: The bowl at the back of the church, marked "For the sick," is for monetary donations only.

OUR CHURCH TODAY

*I*f you do not have a hymnal, please steal one from an empty pew.

April 26

Gerry hit Father Dave with a theological baseball question. "Who does God root for when the Padres play the Angels?"

September 20

*T*uesday at 4:00 P.M., we will be serving homemade ice cream. All ladies giving milk please come early.

April 27

TODAY'S SERVICE

The third verse of "Amazing Grace" will be sung without musical accomplishment.

September 19

"These kids see way too many movies," one Sunday school teacher told another. "Now they think Jonah should have been saved from the whale by Nemo."

April 28

"*I*'m pleased to report we finally found a plumber for the church washroom," Reverend Wes told the congregation. "And now, let us sing: 'O Happy Day.'"

After the church service, Billy told the pastor, "When I grow up, I'm going to give you some money. My daddy says you're one of the poorest preachers we've ever had."

April 29

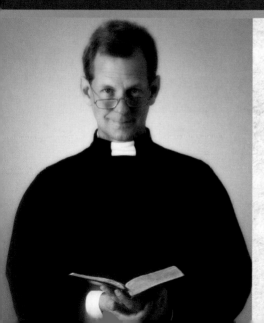

The deceased was a grouch and hated everybody. The minister skirted this point as kindly as he could when he opened the funeral service by saying, "Nearly beloved...."

September 17

CHURCH EVENTS

The fall Council Retreat will be hell September 20 and 21.

SERVICE NOTES

The congregation is asked to remain seated until the end of the recession.

September 16

"*T*here are girl angels,"
May told her brother.
"Their names are Cher
Ubim and Sarah Phim."

May 1

The Optometrist's Hymn:
"Open My Eyes that I
Might See Thee"

September 15

Reverend Vicky was asked to perform some baptisms for a traveling circus, so she took the clowns down to the river for a fool immersion.

May 2

Tina was having a little difficulty with her prayer: "Give us this day our deli bread! Glory be to the Father and to the Son and to the Whole East Coast."

September 14

THE MORNING SERMON:
Women in the Church

THE EVENING SERMON:
Rise Up, O Men of God

May 3

CHURCH NOTES

The blessing of the pets will be held this Sunday. Bowls, collars, and leashes will be sold for a small flea.

OUR CHURCH
TODAY

*R*emember the Children's Ministry Bake Sale. Our kids make great snacks.

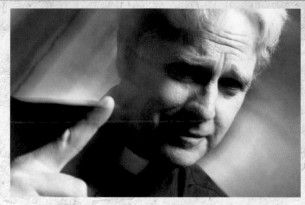

Reverend Jake was well known for his odd metaphors:
"Just because your pants are blessed doesn't mean
you don't need a Bible belt."

September 12

Dear Pastor,
Are there any
devils on earth?
I think there
may be one in
my class.

CARLA, AGE 8

May 5

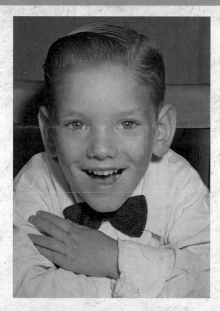

Tommy asked if he could send his dad's boss a copy of the Old Testament. When asked why, Tommy replied, "Because he told my dad they weren't going to have any prophets this year."

VOLUNTEER OPPORTUNITIES

We also need a few more volunteers to help with monthly potlucks due to the large members attending.

May 6

"Do you think my friend Mary Catherine goes to a different church every week?" Missy asked her mom. "She told me she was a roaming Catholic."

September 10

"Who discovered what many believe are the original writings of the Bible?" asked the teacher.

Donna raised her hand and said, "The Dead Sea Trolls?"

May 7

*B*efore viewing slides from the pastor's recent conference, the choir will sing "O God, We Ask for Strength."

September 9

"Let us bow our heads in prayer for the many who
are sick of our church and community."

May 8

A preacher ended his temperance sermon by saying, "The world would be a better place if everyone poured their beer, wine, and whiskey into the river." Then he sat down. The song leader stood and announced with a smile, "For our closing song, let us sing Hymn 365: 'Shall We Gather at the River.'"

The Realtor's Hymn:
"I've Got a Mansion,
Just over the Hilltop"

Deacon Don always knew how to raise money. While sitting in a dunking booth at the church picnic, he doubled his contributions just by wearing a sign that said "Goliath."

September 7

Dear God,
My brothers told me about being born, but it doesn't sound right. They are just kidding, aren't they?

MARSHA, AGE 9

May 10

CHURCH HAPPENINGS

Remember the youth department rummage sale to raise funds for summer camp. We have a Gents three-speed bicycle, also two ladies for sale, in good running order.

September 6

A grandmother read Bible stories to her grandson, Paul. She read, "The man named Lot was warned to take his wife and flee out of the city, but his wife looked back and turned to salt."

Paul asked, "What happened to the flea?"

May 11

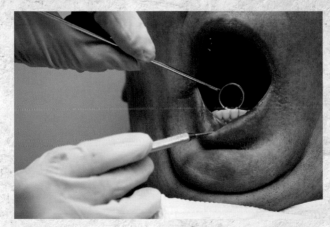

The Dentist's Hymn: "Crown Him with Many Crowns"

September 5

Reverend Jack gets pretty frustrated with the teens in his Bible study class, especially when they ask if the e-pistles were e-mails from God.

May 12

Dear Pastor,
My father says
I should learn the
Ten Commandments.
But I don't think I
want to because we
already have enough
rules in our house.

CHRIS, AGE 6

September 4

Take the time today to smile at someone who is hard to love. Say "hell" to someone who doesn't care much about you.

May 13

OUR CHURCH TODAY

*I*n order to defray the cost of church-yard maintenance, it would be appreciated if those who are willing would clip the grass around their own graves.

September 3

"Why did Jesus choose 12 apostles?" the Sunday school teacher asked.

"So his softball team would have a couple of extra pitchers?" Ben speculated.

May 14

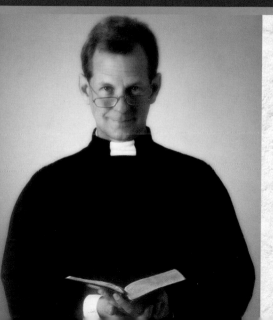

*R*everend Bill had to stop the teen Bible class and explain to one young computer whiz that Emanuel is not an online instruction guide you get when you buy a new PC.

September 2

Reverend Zeke was probably thinking about his fishing trip that afternoon when he said in his sermon: "Let them have dominion over the fish of the sea, and the lake and the river and the pond too."

Mickey told his mom he was afraid the pastor would throw an egg at him because he said in the sermon: "Take my yoke upon you."

September 1

Please place your donation in the envelope along with the deceased person you want remembered.

May 16

SERVICE NOTES

A sermon by the visiting minister will be followed by a luncheon: Attend and you will hear an excellent speaker and heave a great meal.

August 31

After attending Sunday school, Sarah informed her mother that Solomon had 300 wives and 700 porcupines.

May 17

Dear God,
I would like to know
why in the Bible all
the things you said
are in red?

JOANNE, AGE 8

August 30

*E*very shopper in church woke up when the preacher yelled during his sermon: "And the Wal-Marts of Jericho came tumbling down!"

May 18

CHURCH EVENTS

The high schoolers will be presenting Shakespeare's *Hamlet* in the church basement Friday at 7:00 P.M. The congregation is invited to attend this tragedy.

August 29

Dear God,
I bet it is very hard for you to love every-body in the whole world. There are only four people in our family, and I can never do it.

JULIE, AGE 8

May 19

"CPR classes will be held in the church hall next Saturday," the deacon announced. "And now let us close by singing: 'Lord, Send a Revival.'"

August 28

CHURCH EVENTS

Low-self-esteem support group will meet Thursday at 7:00 P.M. Please use the back door.

May 20

A Sunday school teacher asked his class, "Does anyone know what we mean by sins of omission?" One of the girls replied, "Aren't those the sins we should have committed but didn't?"

August 27

The football-loving minister caught the coin he flipped and said to the congregation, "You've won the toss and elected to receive the Holy Spirit!"

May 21

VOLUNTEER OPPORTUNITIES

We are looking for new members for our Community Stewardship Group. Next Saturday at 11:00 A.M. we will meet at Will Rogers Park to eat and collect garbage.

Mrs. Roberts will be serving salad without dressing at this afternoon's potluck lunch.

May 22

"Many thanks to those members who donated lightbulbs for the new church offices," the minister said to the congregation. "And now let us sing: 'I Saw the Light.'"

CHURCH NOTES

*D*ue to complaints from some of the other teams, the head of the interfaith softball league has asked that we stop scoring triples as a "holy trinity."

May 23

CHURCH NOTES

The peacekeeping meeting scheduled for today has been canceled due to a conflict.

August 24

Reverend Mel's mom knew he would become a preacher when she heard him say while playing checkers, "Hearken unto their voice, and make them a king."

"*F*ather Hans is the pastor of our mission parish in Bavaria," said Father Vic. "I like to think of him as our German Shepherd."

August 23

When asked what he had learned in Sunday school, Jeremy replied, "Adam and Eve were created from an apple tree."

May 25

When Jimmy's mother asked him what he had learned in Sunday school, Jimmy replied, "Jesus was big on the golden rule, which says to do one to others before they do one to you."

August 22

Tonight's sermon topic is "What Is Hell?" Come early and listen to our choir practice.

May 26

CHURCH HAPPENINGS

The agenda was adopted … the minutes were approved … the financial secretary gave a grief report.

August 21

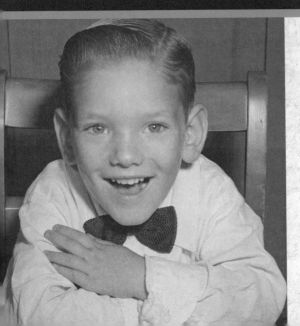

After Sunday school, Marcus reported to his parents, "Syntax is all the money collected at the church from sinners."

May 27

"There were giants on the earth in those days," the preacher read from Genesis.

From the back, a voice asked, "San Francisco or New York?"

August 20

Part-time secretary needed to answer church phone
and give massages to the pastor.

May 28

Dear Pastor,
Our father should be
a minister. Every duy
he gives us a sermon
about something.

Michael, age 7
Aron, age 9

August 19

Asked to recite the Ten Commandments, Tommy said, "Well, I don't remember the first four, but the Fifth Commandment is humor thy father and mother."

May 29

"What book of the Bible should I read before bungee jumping?" asked Clyde.

"Luke," replied the quick-thinking minister. "You should always Luke before you leap."

*D*uring a sermon, Eric leaned over to his brother and whispered, "When the blind lead the blind, you better just get out of the way."

May 30

Let us pray for Harold Johnson, who has been suffering from severe depression ever since joining our congregation.

August 17

One night Mike's parents overheard this prayer: "Now I lay me down to rest, I hope I pass tomorrow's test. If I should die before I wake, that's one less test I have to take. Amen."

*R*everend Martha came up with a list of no-nos for the church camping trip. She called them her Tent Command-ments.

August 16

VOLUNTEER OPPORTUNITIES

*H*elpers are needed!
Please sign up on the
volunteer sheep.

June 1

CHURCH NOTES

Bertha Belch, a missionary from Africa, will be speaking tonight at Calvary Methodist. Come hear Bertha Belch all the way from Africa.

"*P*lease page your brother," Mom asked Joel.

"Why?" he asked. "Am I my brother's beeper?"

Deacon Oscar used to be a weather reporter, which explains why his favorite hymn is "Lo, He Comes with Clouds Descending."

August 14

Dear God,
If we come back
as something, please
don't let me come
back as Donna
Rogers, because
I hate her.

DENNIS, AGE 5

June 3

Dear God,
Of all the people who
worked for you, I like
Noah and David best.

Rob, age 7

VOLUNTEER OPPORTUNITIES

Please note that a three-year-old teacher is needed for Sunday school. Experience preferred.

June 4

CHURCH HAPPENINGS

Talent Show next Saturday night.
All interested please sign up after today's
services. No talent required.

August 12

Robbie drew a picture of Abraham carrying a light-bulb. He told his teacher, "It's for the sacrificial lamp."

June 5

Dear God,
Did you mean for the giraffe to look like that, or was it an accident?

NORMA, AGE 7

August 11

*D*iana and Dan
request your presents
at their wedding.

June 6

SERVICE NOTES

The Reverend Merriwether spoke briefly, much to the delight of the audience.

August 10

For God so loved the world that He did not send a committee.

June 7

Lynn spent the entire ride home from church inspecting the bottom of her shoe. She finally put it back on and told her mom, "I know why Reverend Ron told us to do some sole searching. I found gum, tape, and a bug on mine!"

Melissa returned from Sunday school and reported, "Moses died before he reached Canada."

June 8

OUR CHURCH TODAY

Please join us as we show our support for Josh and Bridget in preparing for the girth of their child.

August 8

CHURCH EVENTS

I want to remind the choir and all special sinners to be at the park by 4:30 P.M. for warmup and sound checks.

June 9

Dear God,
In Sunday school
they told us what
you do. But who
does it when you
are on vacation?

JILL, AGE 10

Dear God,
We read that Thomas Edison made light. But in Sunday school, we learned that you did it. I bet he stole your idea.

MICHAEL, AGE 9

CHURCH NOTES

We now have a Lost & Found.
If you have lost anything please
place it in the big, green box in the
administrative office.

August 6

The shoppers at the kitchen supply store cracked up as little Scott marched around carrying a utensil holder while singing: "A mighty fork rest is our God."

*J*ason scolded his dad for helping a neighbor paint his house. He told him: "The commandment says 'Thou shalt not cover thy neighbor's house!'"

August 5

SERVICE NOTES

*T*here's a sign-up sheet for anyone wishing to be water baptized on the table in the foyer.

June 12

Let us pray for the teens in our church who will spend their summer in Bible Camp.

August 4

*B*obby knew exactly what Jesus would drive: "A van that seats 12 and can pull a boat."

June 13

Peter put a robe and a gray beard on the leader of his toy soldier troop. He called them "Moses and the Ten Commandos."

*F*ather Dan liked to throw a multicultural flair into wedding ceremonies by telling the happy couple to "love, honor, and olé!"

June 14

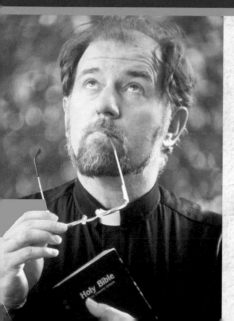

Pictures from the seminary picnic are now available. Anyone thinking about becoming a priest should see Father Bill, who will share his negatives.

CHURCH NOTES

Are you 45 and getting nowhere? Why not consider the Christian ministry?

"God should have asked Michael to save the animals," Darrel told his mom, "because he's an ark angel."

Dear God,
If you give me a genie lamp
like Aladdin, I will give you
anything you want, except
my money or my chess set.

RAPHAEL, AGE 9

June 16

*D*eacon Steve is our church's Internet preacher.
His sermons are always filled with references
to e-commerce, e-mail, and e-pistles.

July 31

Our eighth grade students are enjoying the second half of their two-week trip to Japan. Please pray for our euthanasia.

Little Pat watched a minister wash his hands in a public restroom. "He's not a man of the cloth," he told his dad. "He used the hand dryer."

July 30

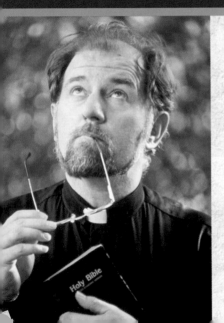

When asked to explain his job, the minister said, "The Lord is the Great Physician, and I'm His HMO."

June 18

ACKNOWLEDGMENTS

A new loudspeaker system has been installed in the church. It was given by one of our members in honor of his wife.

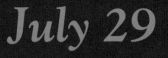

"*I*'ll bet Moses had a hard time hiring people," Sam said, "especially after he turned his staff into a snake."

June 19

Trying to convince his mom he should get an allowance every day instead of once a week, Tommy told his mom, "Jesus wants me to get an allowance every day. That's why the Lord's Prayer says 'Give us this day our daily bread.'"

After sampling the many delicious bean casseroles at the potluck dinner, the choir sang "There's a Song in the Air."

June 20

Today's blessing of the pets will be followed by the "Sermon on the Mouse."

July 27

After listening to his older sister talk on her cell phone for hours, Tyler started calling the nearby cellular phone tower the Tower of Babble.

June 21

You could tell Father Jim was happy with his sermon because he ended by saying, "Many have yawned, but few are dozin'."

For Sale:
suits, pants,
dresses!

CHURCH EVENTS

Vintage clothing sale this Saturday in the church basement. Stop by and check out the satan dresses.

June 22

OUR CHURCH TODAY

The associate minister unveiled the church's new tithing campaign slogan last Sunday: "I Upped My Pledge— Up Yours."

July 25

John and Susan have been lifelong friends. This marriage marks the end of that friendship.

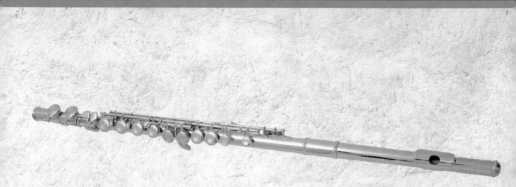

"*E*ve must have been a really bad musician," said Kenny to his dad. "That's why God told her about the forbidden flute."

July 24

We have enough prizes for the games, but we still need some volunteers to run the barbecue for the church carnivore.

June 24

CHURCH HAPPENINGS

This evening at 7:00 there will be a hymn sing in the park across from the church. Bring a blanket and come prepared to sin.

July 23

When a bulb burned out during church services, Janet looked up and commented, "Looks like they need an acolyte."

June 25

Matt wrote down all the things he wanted to do before the end of the world. He called it his "apoca-list."

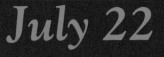

MEMBERSHIP OPPORTUNITIES

This Sunday, the Cragg's son Taylor will be circus sized. All wishing to bear witness are welcome.

June 26

Next Sunday a special collection will be taken to defray the cost of the new carpet. All those wishing to do something on the new carpet will come forward and do so at that time.

July 21

The pastor's wife asked little Linda if she had a boyfriend. Linda replied, "Nope. I'm like Jesus— I love them all."

June 27

Dear Pastor,
I liked your sermon
on Sunday. Especially
when it was finished.

MARIE, AGE 7

CHURCH NEWS

The parking lot has been repainted. We're asking all children in the parish to help their parents stay inside the lines.

June 28

CHURCH EVENTS

The Seniors' group is sponsoring a picnic this Saturday. Each person is asked to bring a friend, a vegetable, or a dessert in a covered dish.

July 19

Dear God,
We had a good time at church today. Wish you could have been there.

MATTHEW, AGE 7

June 29

*L*adies, don't forget the rummage sale. It is a good chance to get rid of those things not worth keeping around the house. Bring your husbands.

"I don't think this milk is good," Mom told Billy.

"Maybe it needs to go to church," he replied.

June 30

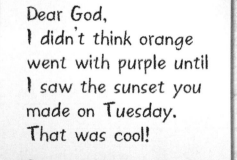

Dear God,
I didn't think orange went with purple until I saw the sunset you made on Tuesday. That was cool!

SEAN, AGE 4

July 17

VOLUNTEER OPPORTUNITIES

The choir is sponsoring a canned goods drive. Please participate and bring your can to church.

July 1

After today's services, the choir will meet in the rehearsal room next to the restrooms to practice a new hymn: "Who Is He in Yonder Stall?"

July 16

During the marriage ceremony poor little Meredith was seated next to a guest who was in need of some deodorant. Meredith wrinkled her nose and said, "Pee-yew! You should have gone to the wedding shower!"

July 2

Dear God,
Who draws the lines
around the countries?

NAN, AGE 9

July 15

Dear God,
My brother is a
rat. You should
give him a tail.

PATRICK, AGE 7

July 3

We continue to apologize for our broken air conditioner. Please join us for hot coffee and toasted bagels immediately following the services.

July 14

A six-year-old was overheard reciting the Lord's Prayer in church: "And forgive us our trash passes, as we forgive those who passed trash against us."

July 4

Dear Pastor,
Could you please
say a prayer for our
Little League team?
We either need God's
help or a new
pitcher.

TIM, AGE 11

July 13

Couples celebrating anniversaries are eligible for marriage vow removal.

July 5

OUR CHURCH TODAY

The windows in the church have been replaced with bullet-proof glass. It is now ready for weddings again.

July 12

After listening to relatives talk at her great-aunt's funeral, Sondra made a list of all the things she owned and who they should go to if she died, then taped a piece of gum to the bottom. She said it was her "last will and peppermint."

The Scrabble game was interrupted when Junior swallowed an X. "Mom! I think we need to perform an X-orcism," Mary yelled.

July 11

Young Adult Weekend. All singles are invited to spend a weekend in the presence of the Lord and other interesting singles.

July 7

SERVICE NOTES

Latecomers are asked to wait until the service is over to be seated.

July 10

One of the first things Adam and Eve did after leaving Eden was raise Cain.

July 8

"My dad is like Jacob," Kelly told his friends. "He did the laundry while Mom was sick, and now I have a coat of many colors."

July 9

CHURCH NOTES

Only a small number of deceased elders have been sent to us. You can still bring yours to the meeting to be added to the list.